Macrame Christmas Patterns

Beautiful Macrame Patterns For Christmas

Copyright © 2023

All rights reserved.

DEDICATION

The author and publisher have provided this e-book to you for your personal use only. You may not make this e-book publicly available in any way. Copyright infringement is against the law. If you believe the copy of this e-book you are reading infringes on the author's copyright, please notify the publisher at: https://us.macmillan.com/piracy

Macrame Christmas Patterns

Contents

Macrame Christmas Stocking 1

Christmas Macrame Star 15

DIY Macrame Feathers 20

Christmas Wreath 30

DIY Macrame Rainbow 38

DIY Macrame Christmas Tree Ornament 50

DIY Rainbow Macramé Earrings 53

Macrame Christmas Patterns

Macrame Christmas Stocking

Macrame Christmas Patterns

Supplies:

-500' of 3mm cotton rope

-12" wooden dowel

—3mm cotton macrame cord

-1/2 yard of off-white wool felt

—over the door hooks measuring at least 10" from outer hook to outer hook or standing clothes rack similar to this one or this one

-sewing machine and thread (or you can hand stitch everything together)

—sharp tapestry needle

-scissors

-straight pins

1.

Macrame Christmas Patterns

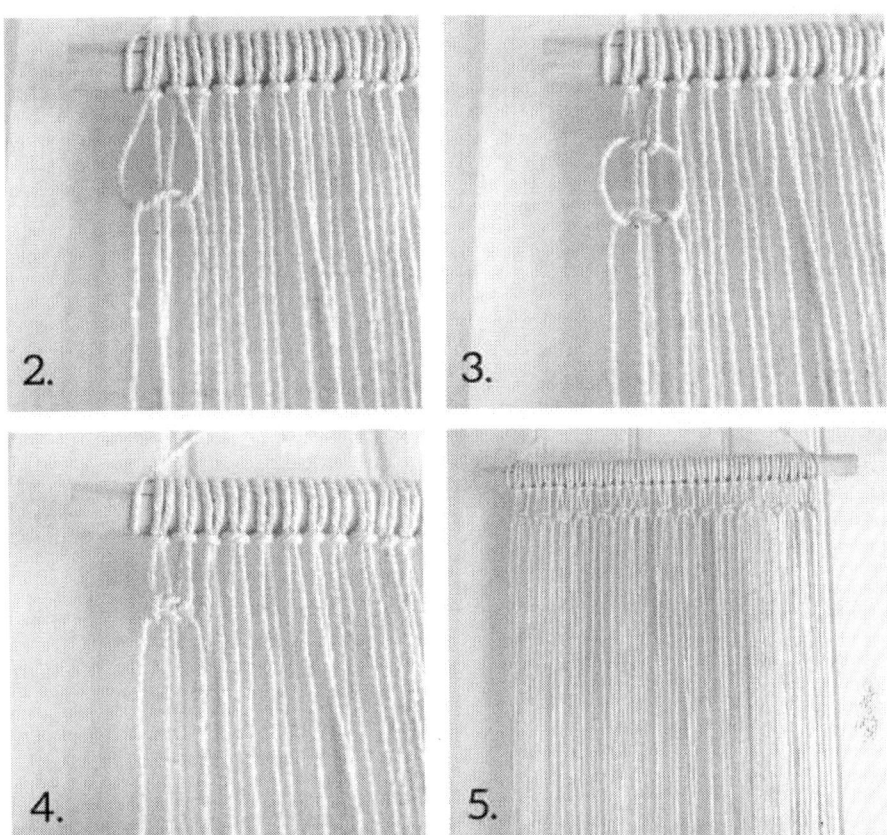

Step One: Cut 30 strands of rope measuring 15' each. Attach each of your 30 strands of 15' rope to your dowel using a lark's head knot (see here). Do your best to attach these so that the ends are even and then space them out evenly along your wooden dowel so that you have about 1" of free space left on each end of your dowel.

Macrame Christmas Patterns

Using your additional piece of rope, tie one end in a double knot on one end of the dowel and the other end on the other end of your dowel to create a hanger. Adjust this to the height you desire so that it's hanging at a comfortable height from your hooks to be able to work on.

Step Two: Using the first four strands on the left side of your dowel, tie a half knot. The two center ropes stay where they are and the two outer ropes pull away just a bit. Then create a bend in the outer left rope and move it towards and then under the outer right rope as shown.

Next, bend the outer right rope under the place where the outer left rope crossed it, behind the two center ropes, and back up through the bend from the outer left rope as shown. Leave about 1/2 of room between the knot and the dowel.

Step Three: Then you'll create another similar half knot but reverse the overlap order of the outer ropes. The outer rope on the right side will go over the center two ropes but under the outer rope on the left side. Then the outer rope on the left side will go behind the center two ropes and come out over the bend in the outer right rope.

Step Four: Pull this second half knot snugly into the first half knot to create a square knot.

Step Five: Repeat steps two through four with the next group of four ropes, and so on, and so on, until you've completed 15 square knots total.

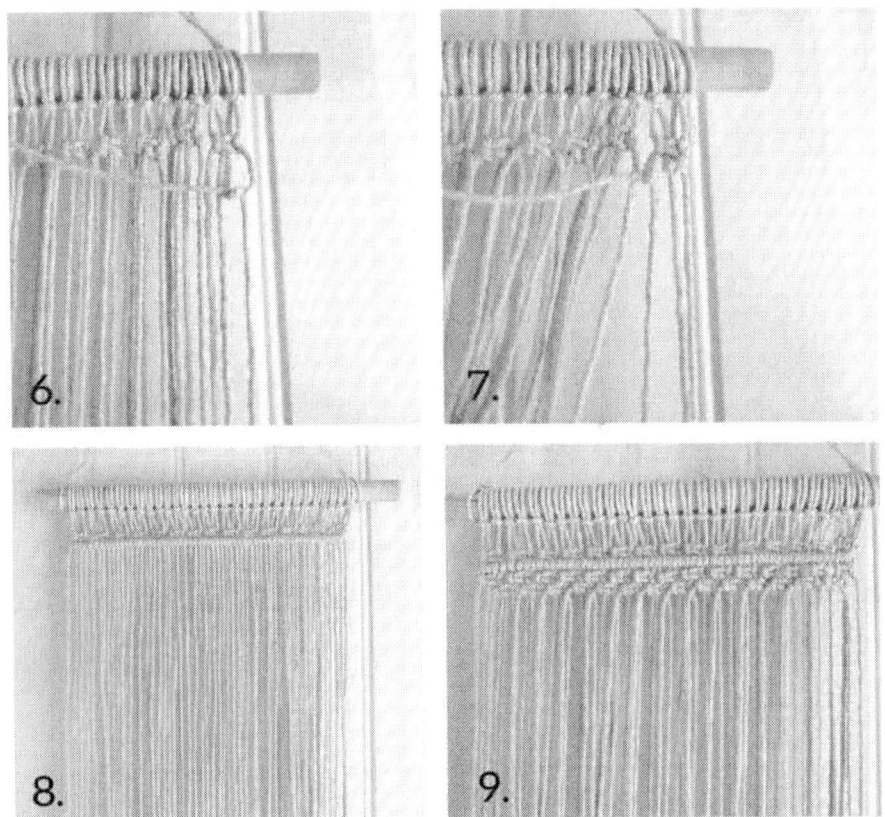

Step Six: Pull the outer right rope across the front of all the other ropes (to the left) and drape the end on a coat hook. This is going to be the base for the next row of single knots that will create a horizontal row. Use the second rope from the right side to tie a single knot around the rope you just draped across.

Step Seven: Then use the third rope from the outside and tie a single knot so that it's snug against the other knot. Then repeat with the fourth rope from the outside and tie a single knot so that it's snug, etc. You'll start to see the pattern.

Step Eight: Continue tying consecutive ropes in a single knot all the way across. You don't want this to be so tight that it pulls the width in at the edges.

Step Nine: Follow this with another 15 square knots snugly under your horizontal row. Then create a second row of square knots by skipping the first two outer rows of rope on the left side before continuing your pattern of square knots using four ropes each. This is called an alternating square knot. It will leave you with two extra ropes on the right side as well.

Step Ten: After four rows of square knots and alternating square knots, you'll create your first diamond. It also kind of looks like a mid-century ornament! You'll use 12 strands of rope on the right side of your piece. Pull all the other non-working ropes off to the side to keep things from getting too tangled.

Wrap the sixth rope from the left over the seventh row from the left using a double half hitch knot (two single knots). This will create the top point of your diamond.

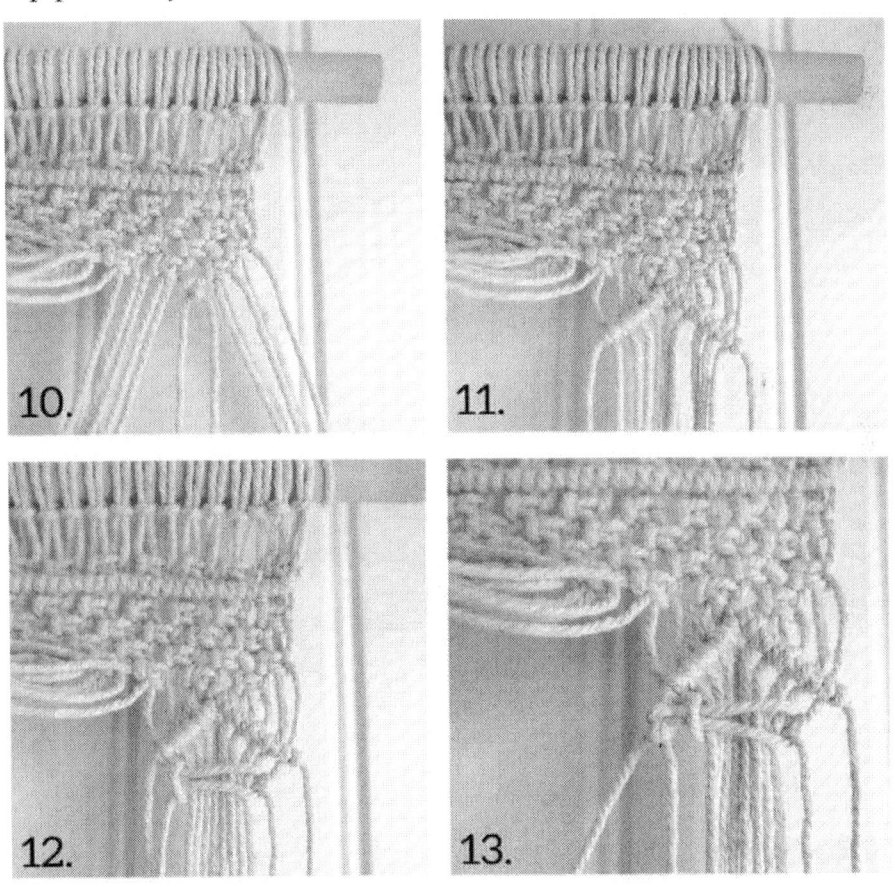

Step Eleven: Wrap the fifth, fourth, third, second, and first ropes around the seventh rope using the same double half hitch knots to create the top right side of the diamond.

Then wrap the eighth, ninth, 10th, 11th, and 12th ropes around the sixth rope using the double half hitch knot to create the top left side of your diamond.

Step Twelve: Use the 11th rope and the second rope from the right side to tie a square knot around all of the ropes in between. Don't pull too tightly—you just want them to rest against the edges so they all have room to breathe.

Step Thirteen: The 12th rope will be the rope you wrap the 11th rope around with a double half hitch. This will create the elbow of the diamond on the left side.

Step Fourteen: Then wrap the 10th, ninth, eighth, and seventh rope around the 12th to finish off the bottom left side fo the diamond. Next, you'll wrap the second, third, fourth, fifth, and sixth around the first rope using the double half hitch to finish off your bottom right side of the diamond.

Step Fifteen: To create the bottom point, wrap the new sixth rope from the right side around the new seventh rope using a double half

Macrame Christmas Patterns

hitch.

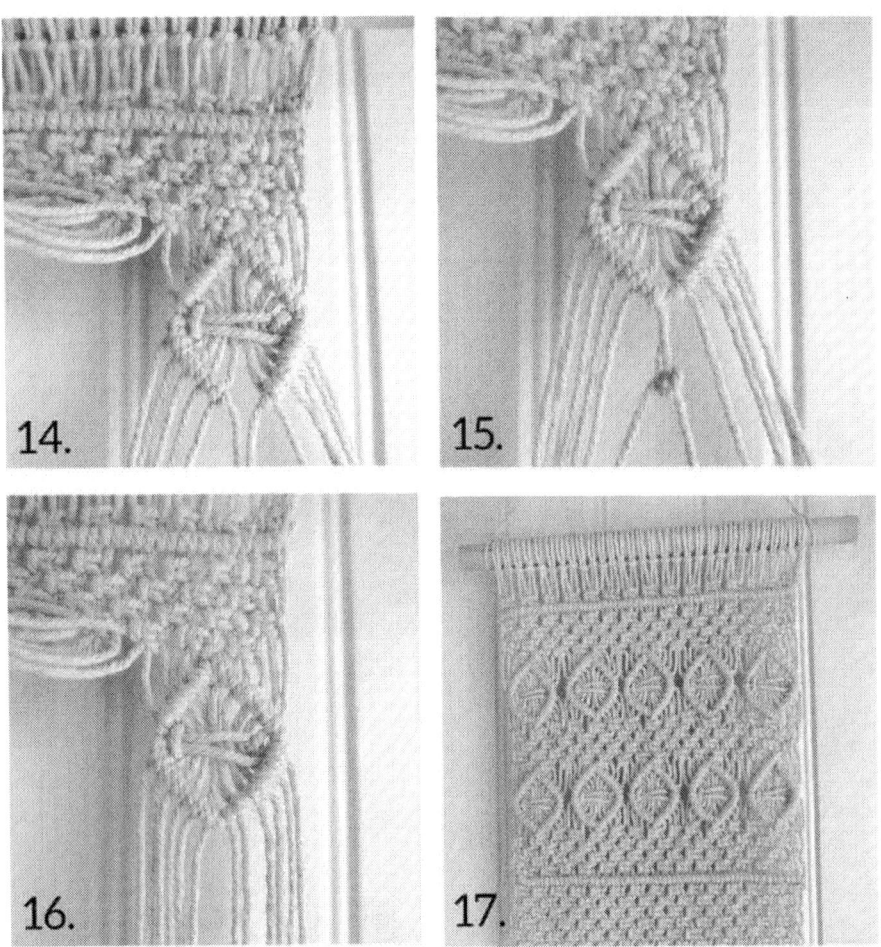

Step Sixteen: This is how your finished diamond will look. You did it!

Step Seventeen: Now finish up the next four diamonds in this row. Next, add four more rows of square knots and alternating square knots before another full row of diamonds. Then another section of four rows of square and alternating square knots as shown. Finally, add another horizontal line as in steps six through eight.

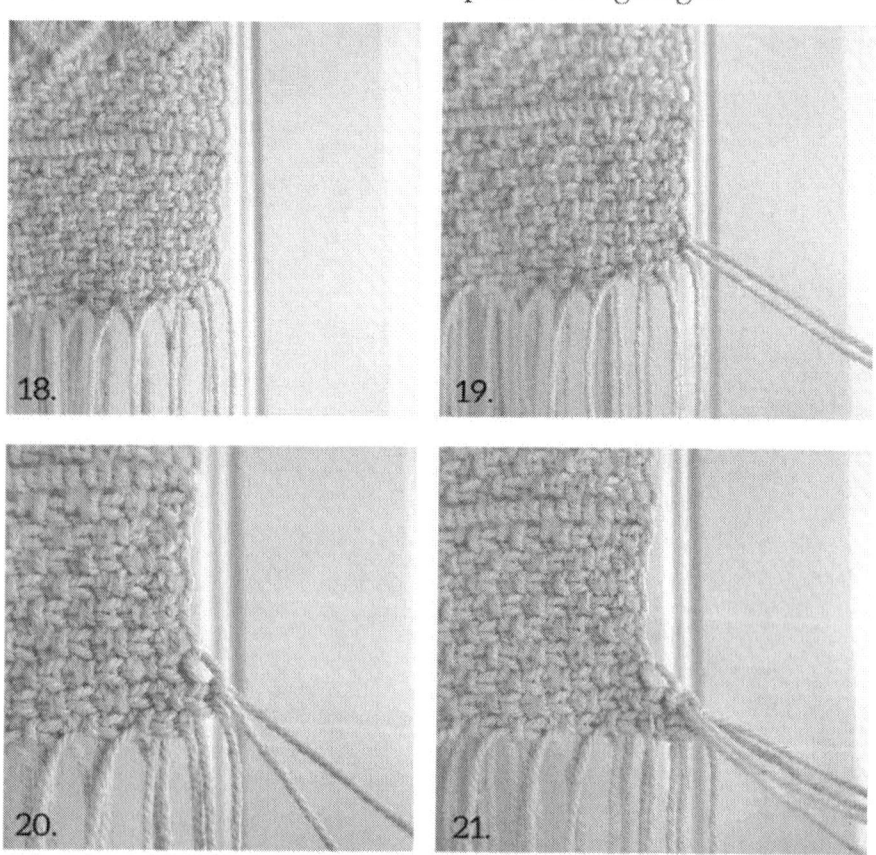

Macrame Christmas Patterns

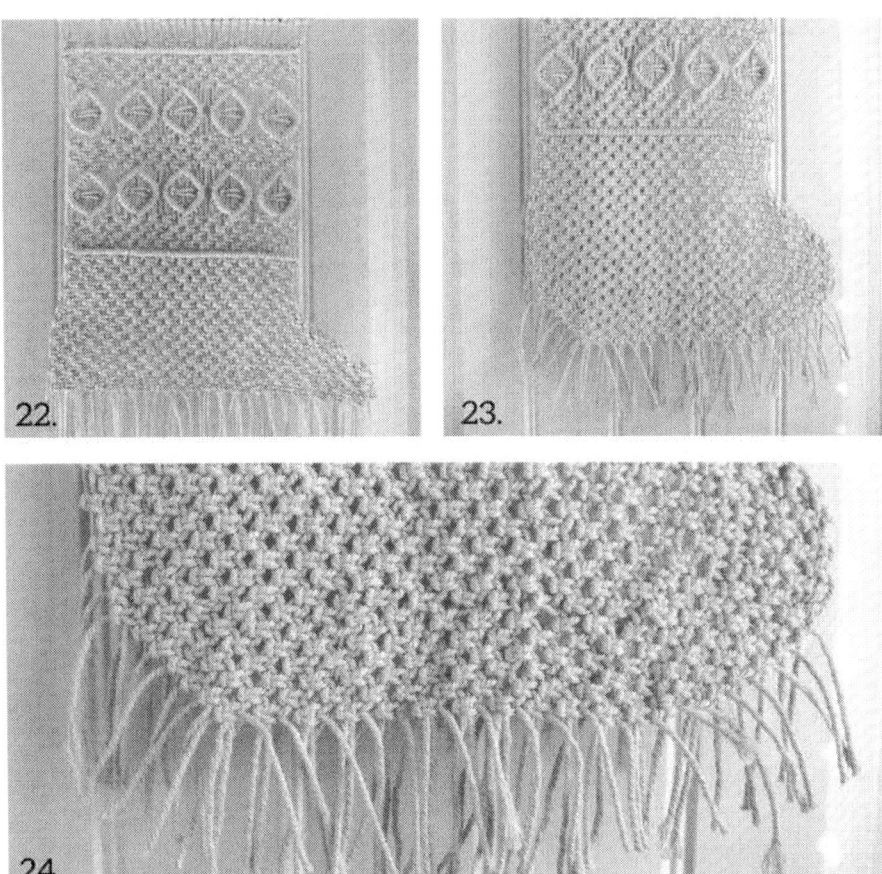

Step Eighteen: Tie eight more rows of square knots and alternating square knots. This is where we'll increase the silhouette for the foot. You should have two extra ropes on the right side.

Step Nineteen: Slip a 4' section of rope through the loop above the two extra ropes on the right side. Center it so that you've got two more strands of rope to use. Then use your four free ropes to tie another square knot in the eighth row.

Step Twenty: Tie a ninth row of square knots all the way across from the left to the right. This will still leave you with an additional two rope strands on the right side. So, add another 4' section of rope through the loop above the two extra ropes on the right just like in step 19. This introduction of new strands will increase the width of your stocking to start the toe shape.

Step Twenty-One: Once you've finished your ninth row, add two strands of 4' rope through the loop above the outer knot. This will widen your stocking even further for a more distinguished toe shape.

Step Twenty-Two: Continue steps 19 through 21 until you've finished a total of 14 rows of square and alternating square knots. Each even row should get an additional two strands of rope and each odd row should have only two strands of rope added. Rows 15 through 19 should be knotted without any additional strands added in.

Step Twenty-Three: The next section of rows will taper in at each side by two ropes on each outer edge. This means rows 20 through

25 will be decreasing on each end by two ropes.

Step Twenty-Four: Here's a close up of the bottom section. You'll have much shorter ropes to work with at this point! We suggest trimming them down to about 2" for now. If they get too short, they may start unraveling.

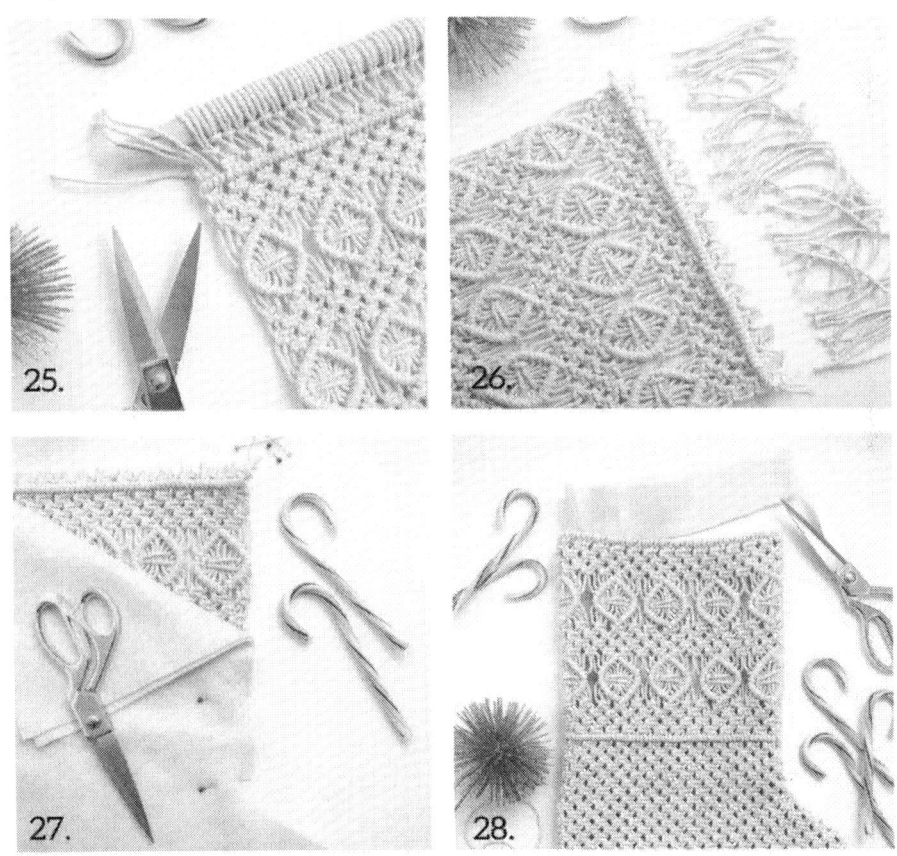

Step Twenty-Five: Let's get this piece off of your dowel. Loosen the lark's head knots and cut them off.

Step Twenty-Six: Trim your rope strands so that there is only about 1/2" above the first row of square knots.

Step Twenty-Seven: Place your finished macrame piece on top of two pieces of wool felt. Choose this fiber because you don't need to worry about unraveling or adding a hem on the back side. Plus, it feels extra cozy in your hands. Use the macrame piece as your template and cut out the same shape in the two pieces of wool with about 1/2" of room around the perimeter.

Put both pieces of wool on top of the macrame piece and pin all three layers together with straight pins, except for across the top of the stocking. Hand or machine stitch through all three layers all the way from the top right corner, around the toes, around the heel, and back up to the top left corner. Be sure not to stitch the top side shut.

Step Twenty-Eight: Turn right side out so that the macrame layer is on the front. Tuck the square knots at the top inside so that they're between the front of the macrame piece and the middle layer of wool. This will give you a nice clean line at the top. You'll have a little extra wool felt on the top. Trim it down so that it's flush with the top of your macrame piece.

Step Twenty-Nine: With a sharp tapestry needle and thread or leftover rope, stitch the middle piece of felt to the horizontal row of macrame. Be sure to tie a knot where you begin and end. You can use a blanket stitch or a whip stitch, which is where you stitch through both layers from back to front over and over.

Step Thirty: Add a three-inch loop on the left side so you can hang it anywhere you like!

Christmas Macrame Star

You Will Need

- Copper star wreath, from Hobbycraft or craft shop

Macrame Christmas Patterns

- Single twist string (47m), from Greenfibres
- Scissors
- Masking tape
- Measuring Tape
- Pet brush or comb

Total time: An afternoon

Step 1

Cut 146 lengths of string, 30cm each, and one 2.5m length. One by one, tie the shorter strings onto the wreath using the lark's head knot – fold each piece in half, place under the frame and then thread the ends through the loop.

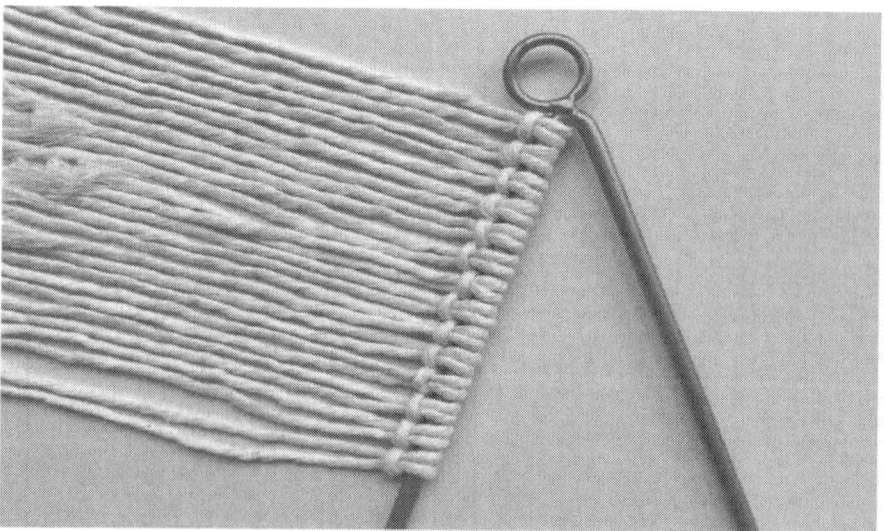

Macrame Christmas Patterns

Step 2

Take your long string, leave a tail of about 8-10 cm and fix it onto a flat surface with some masking tape near the top of the star.

Step 3

Use the long string as a guide and tie your 146 strings on it using the double half hitch knot, going carefully around the bends.

Step 4

Trim the strings at about 8cm. Comb out the string to make a fringe and trim so the ends are even.

Macrame Christmas Patterns

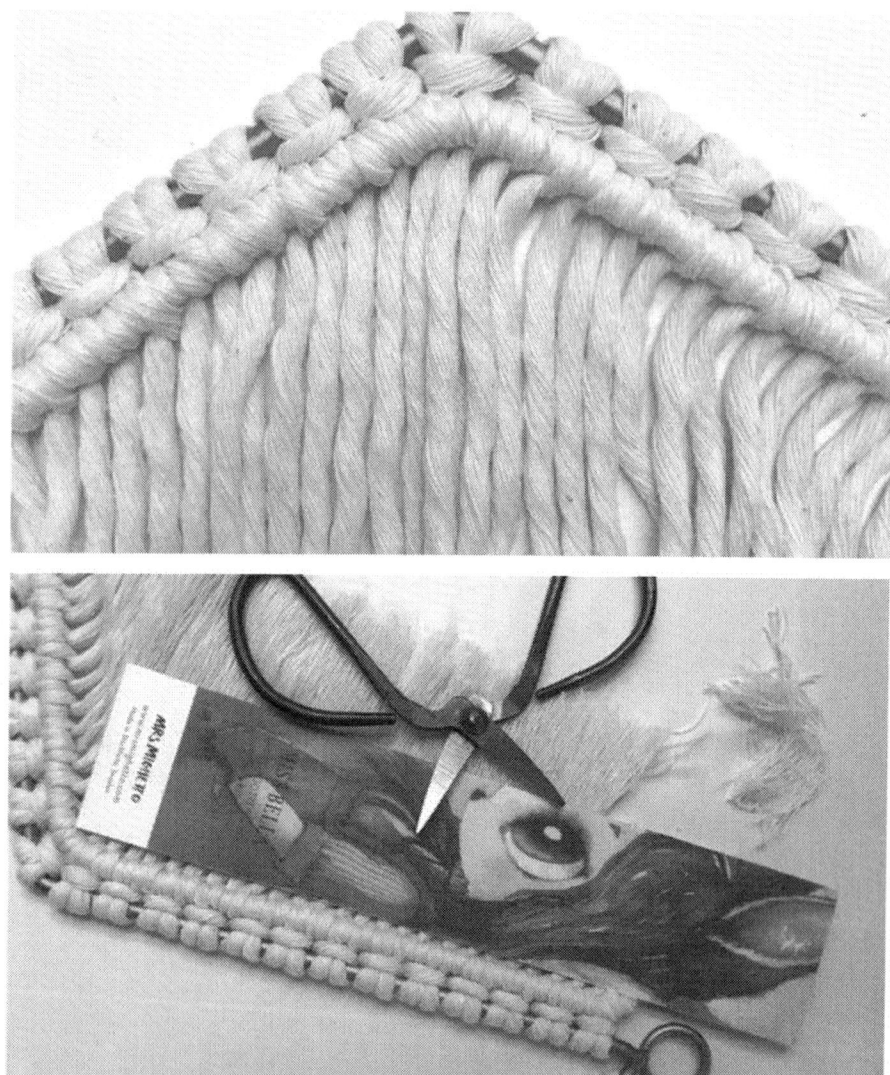

Macrame Christmas Patterns

Step 5

If the fringe is quite long, you can use spray starch to hold it in place.

DIY Macrame Feathers

You'll Need:

- 5mm single twist cotton string
- fabric stiffener
- sharp fabric shears
- cat brush
- ruler

Macrame Christmas Patterns

For a medium sized feather, cut:

- 1 32" strand for the sprine
- 10-12 14" strands for the top
- 8-10 12" strands for the middle
- 6-8 10" strands for the bottom

Fold the 32" strand in half. Take one of the 14" strands, fold it in half and tuck it under the spine.

Macrame Christmas Patterns

Take another 14" strand, fold it in half and insert it into the loop of the top horizontal strand. Pull it through and lay it horizontally, on top of the opposing strand.

Macrame Christmas Patterns

Now pull the bottom strands all the way through the top loop. This is your knot!

Pull both sides tightly. On the next row, you'll alternate the starting side. So if you laid the horizontal strand from left to right the first time, you'll lay the horizontal strand from right to left next.

Lay the first folded strand under the spine, thread another folded strand into its loop. Pull the lower strands through the top loop. And tighten.

Macrame Christmas Patterns

Keep going and work gradually down in size.

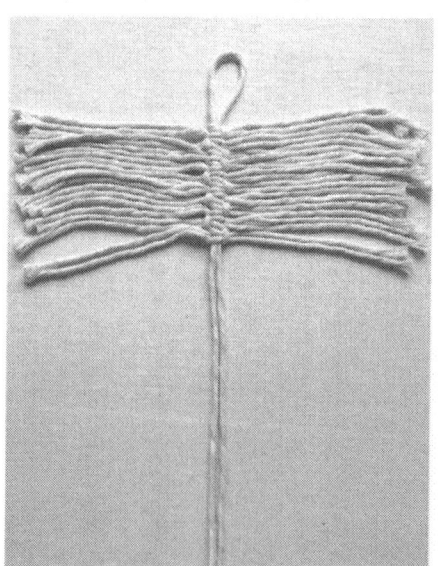
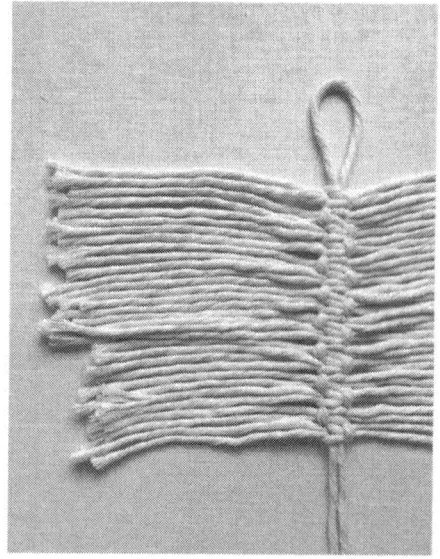

Macrame Christmas Patterns

Be sure to push the strands up to tighten - grab the bottom of the middle (spine) strand with one hand and with another, push the strands up. Once you're done, drag the fringe downwards to meet the bottom of the middle strand.

Then, give it a rough trim. This not only helps guide the shape but also helps with brushing the strands out. The shorter the strands, the easier, to be honest. It also helps to have a very sharp pair of fabric shears!

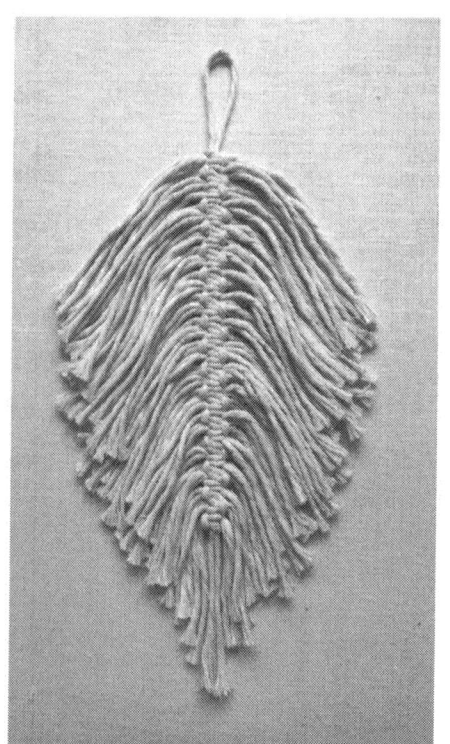 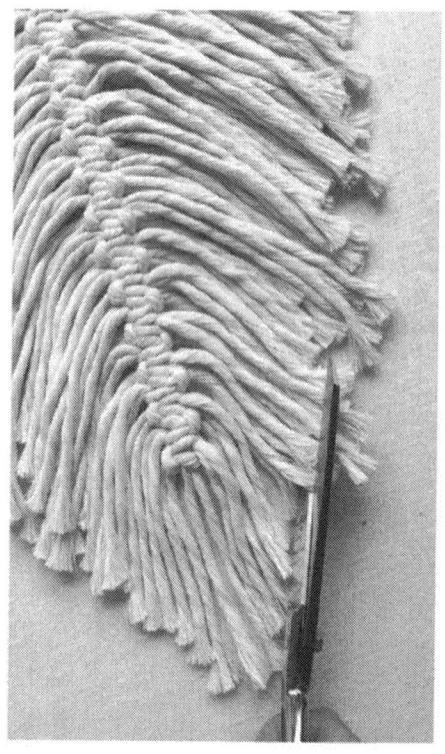

After a rough trim, place the feather on a durable surface as you'll be using an animal brush to brush out the cording. The brush will damage any delicate or wood surface so we suggest using a **self healing cutting mat** or even a flattened cardboard box.

When brushing, start at the spine and push hard into the cording when brushing. It'll take several hard strokes to get that beautiful, soft fringe.

Macrame Christmas Patterns

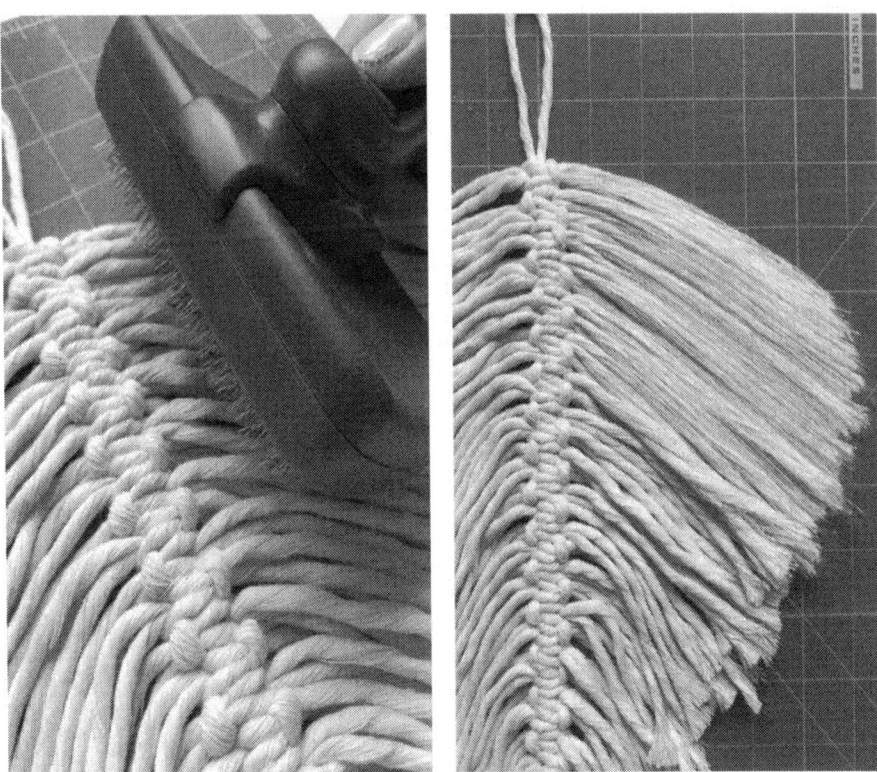

Work your way down. When you're at the bottom, hold the bottom of the spine while brushing - you don't want the brush to yank any strands off!

Next, you'll want to stiffen the feather. The cording is so soft that it'll just flop if you pick it up and try to hang it. Give it spray, or two, and allow to try for at least a couple of hours.

Macrame Christmas Patterns

Once your feather has stiffened up a bit, you can now go back and give it a final trim. This is the most challenging part. Take it easy. It's better to trim less than more! And you might need to adjust your trim depending on how often you're moving the piece. Once you're done trimming, you can even give it another stray of fabric stiffener for good measure. And then, you'll be ready to hang your piece!

Macrame Christmas Patterns

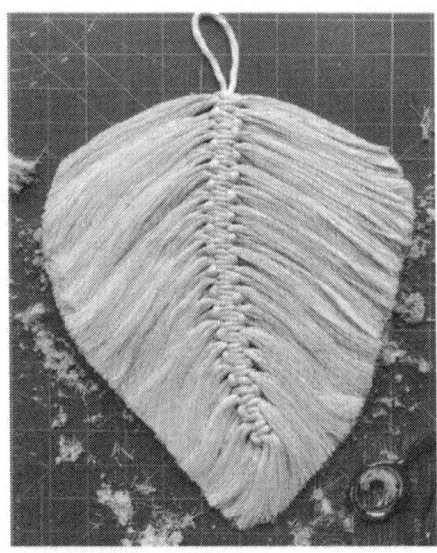

Christmas Wreath

Step 1 :

Cut out 84 strands each 60 cm long.

2nd step :

Macrame Christmas Patterns

Using the lark's head knot technique, install each strand around the ring.

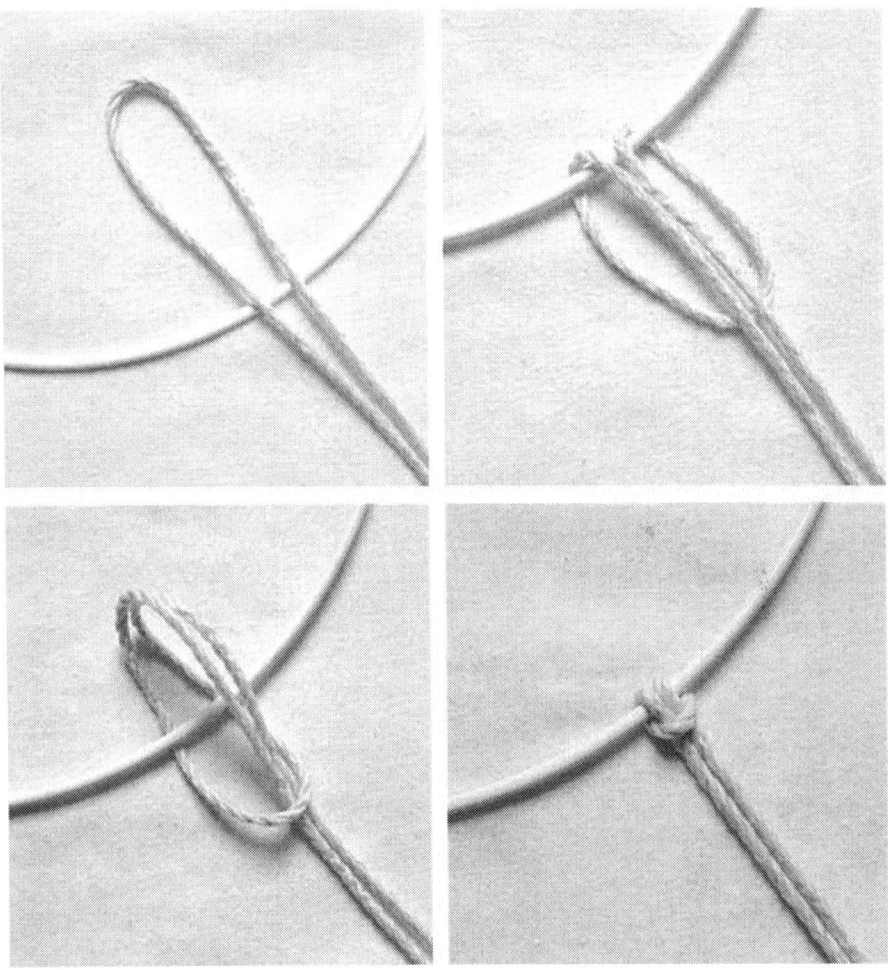

Step 3:

Macrame Christmas Patterns

Once the wires are installed, form a first row of alternating flat knots around the circle: pass the right wire under the two wires of the center and over the wire of left. Then the left wire over the two wires from the center and below the right wire. Tighten the first part of the knot. Pass the left wire under the two middle wires and over the right wire;

Macrame Christmas Patterns

pass the right yarn over the center yarns and below the left yarn. Tighten the 2nd half of the knot.

Step 4:

Form a second row of alternate flat knots.

Step 5:

In the third row, form alternate flat knots by doing the following: * two knots, one space *. Repeat all around the circle

Step 6:

In the fourth row, form alternate flat knots as follows: * two spaces, one knot *. To form triangles.

Step 7:

Macrame Christmas Patterns

Form slanted rod knots under the right side of each triangle. Then under the left side. Finally, connect the two sides. Do this all around the book. Oblique wand node: The wire at the high end of the triangle serves as a guide. Wrap the next thread around the guidewire a first time through below, then in front and then back into the loop obtained. Finally, roll it up again the same way.

Step 8:

Connect each triangle by forming chevrons by making oblique rods knots (see explanation previous step).

Step 9:

Macrame Christmas Patterns

Cut the excess wire, and put a fastener.

Your Christmas wreath is over, you can install it and have a nice holiday season!

DIY Macrame Rainbow

Step One

Gather Materials.

Macrame Christmas Patterns

- 2.4metres of 20mm Twisted Cotton Rope

(You can use other thicknesses however this is great for a sturdy full finish)

- 80m of Art Yarn (this is deliciously soft and fluffy)
- Tape Measure
- Scissors
- A large eye needle, thick enough to thread the chunky yarn through
- A curved needle
- Tape measure
- Sewing thread
- Comb

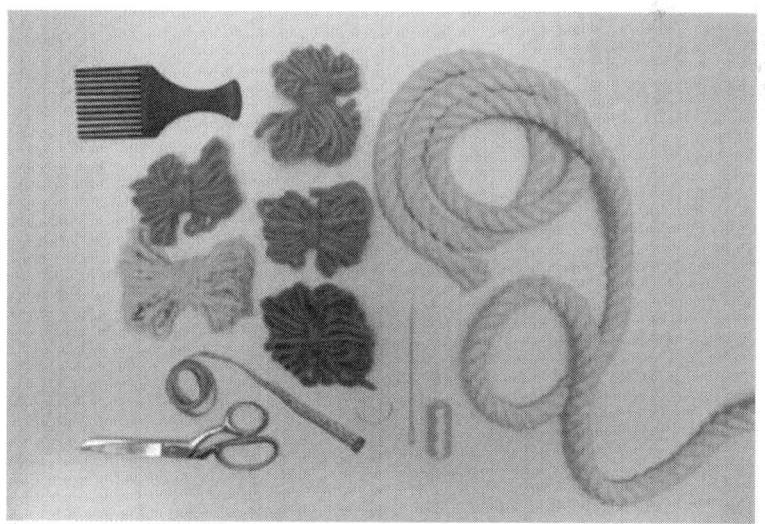

Step Two:

Prepare your fibre materials.

Rope:

Lay it flat to form the shape of a rainbow prior to cutting to avoid waste.

Once you have your shape, cut into x5 pieces.

We will use the following lengths from outside to inside curve in our rainbow.

64cm – 56cm – 48cm – 40cm – 34cm

Thick Yarn:

Choose to use five different colours for a fun effect. This yarn will wrap around you rope to create a textured effect.

We will use the following lengths from outside to inside curve in our rainbow.

14m – 13m – 12m – 11m – 10m

You can use any yarn here, if it is thinner than shown you will need to add additional length, if doing so, its advised to work straight from the ball and not snip your lengths.

Macrame Christmas Patterns

Fibre Materials	Large to-	Curve		Small Curve	-
Rope	64cm	56cm	48cm	40cm	34cm
Yarn	15-18m	13-15m	12-15m	11-13m	10-12m

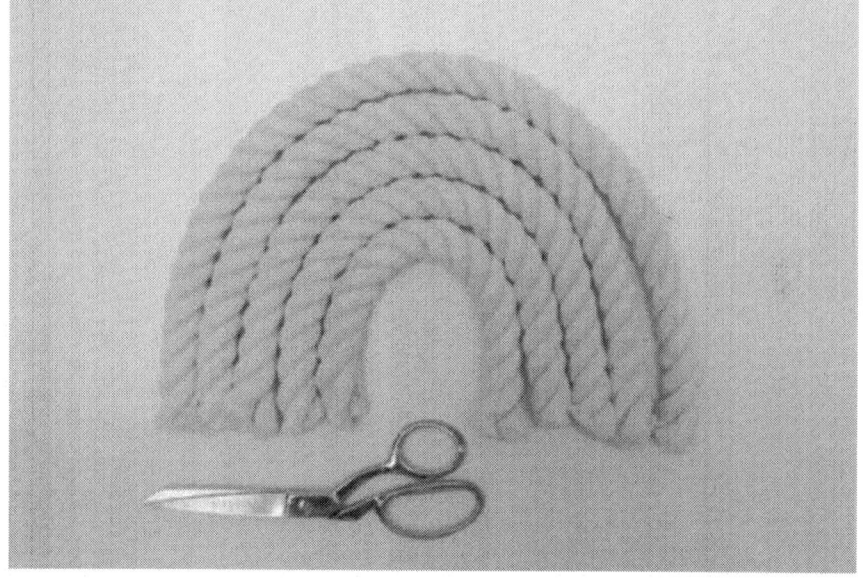

Step Three:

Attaching Yarn to Rope

- Take the fibre materials for your large rainbow curve
- Leave 2cm from the end of your rope and attach your yarn with an overhand knot. Leave the tail facing back towards the rope length.

Take the Yarn in your hand and commence wrapping it firmly 'around and around' around the rope, on top of the yarn tail, covering it up completely.

For best result, ensure that your wrapping technique is neat and consistent.

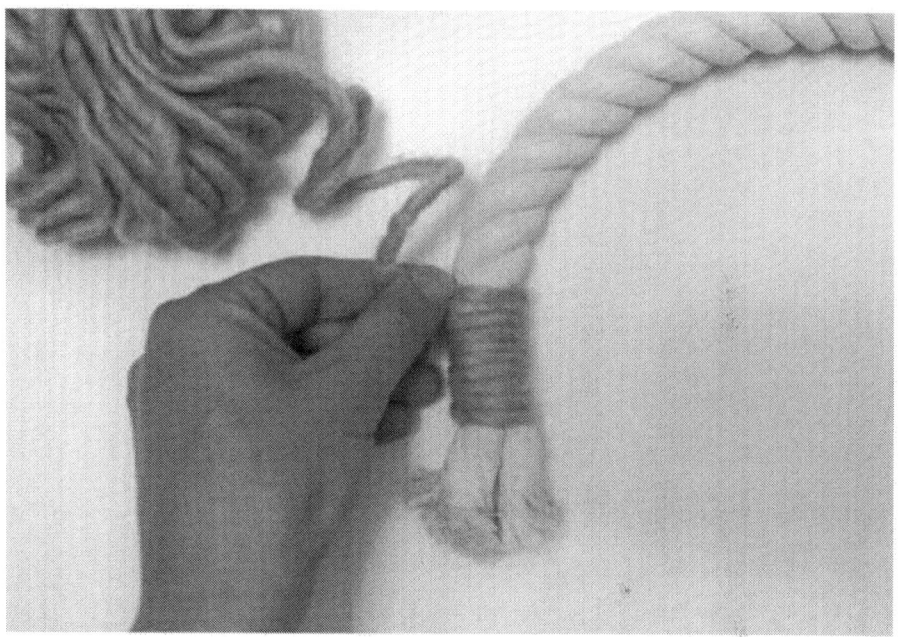

Continue this wrapping technique along the entire length of rope until you comyto the end. Leave a 2cm distance of rope visible.

Thread your yarn through the large eye needle. Sew a stitch back through your last wrapping rotation. Repeat this x3 times to secure your yarn in place.

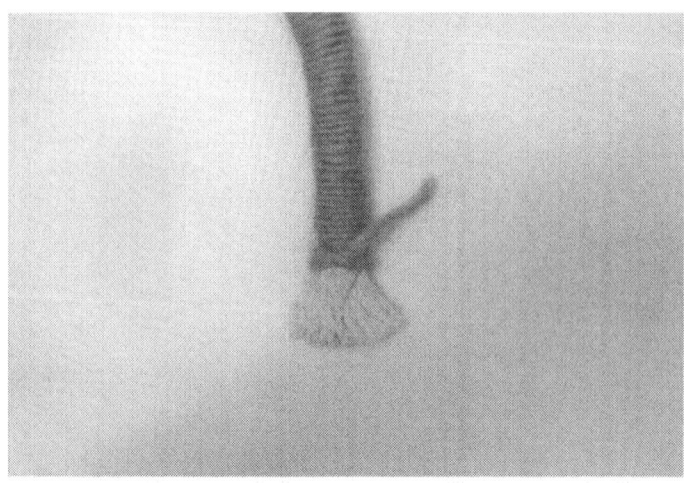

Now thread the needle and yarn back up under and through your rainbow curve, covering around 3-4cm. This hides and secures your yarn. Snip the remaining tail once complete.

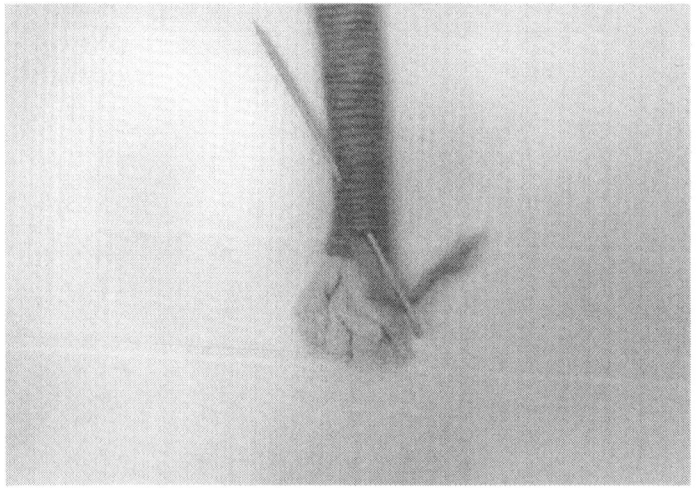

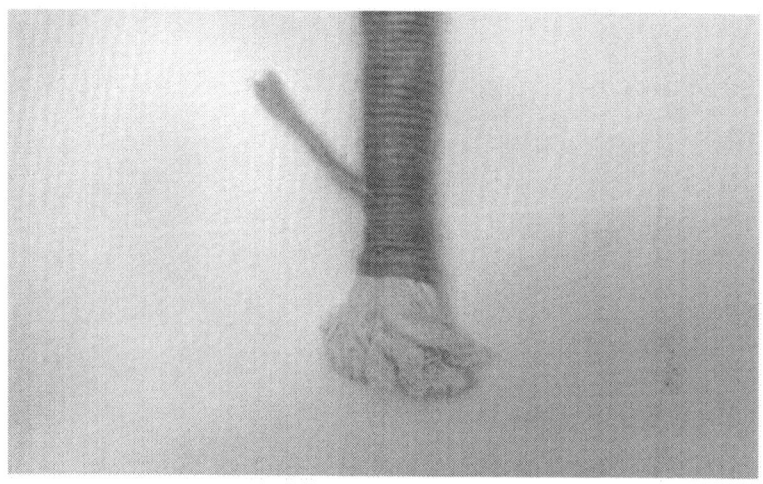

Take your wrapped curve and gently shape it back to its rainbow shape.

You may be able to slightly see your initial overhand knot and the snipped tail; this is the back of your piece and will not be on display.

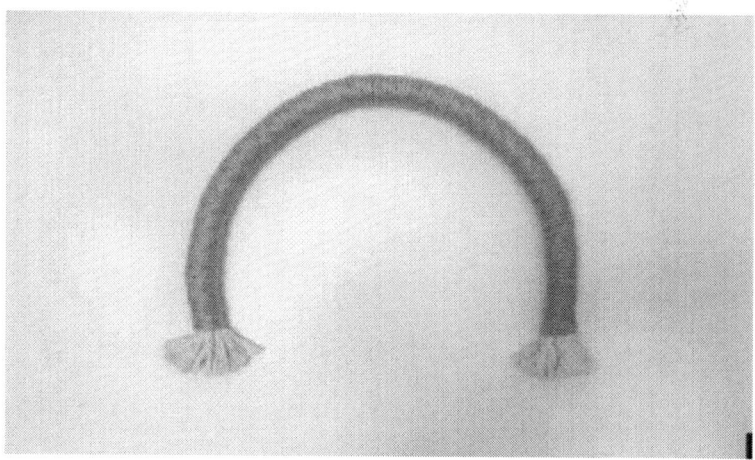

Now we repeat this action, wrapping all five curves. Once complete lay them all together and gently manipulate their resting shape before we sew them together.

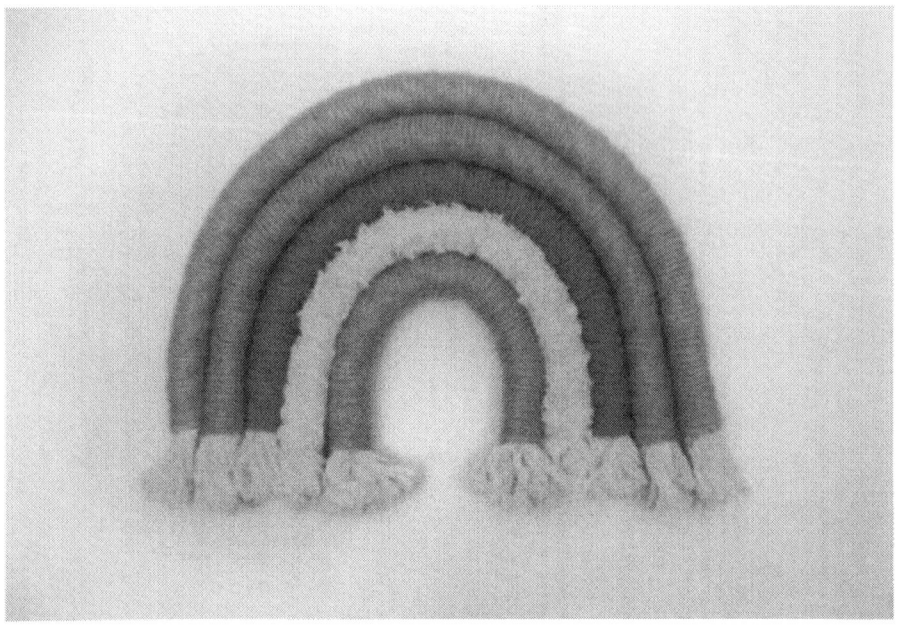

Step Four:

Sewing your curves together

Ensure that you are working on the back of your piece

Take your small curved needle and a length of cotton thread; you will sew every rainbow to its neighbour. Ensure your tension is tight, we wish for the curves to be as close as can be to each other.

Macrame Christmas Patterns

If you do not have a curved needle a regular one will be fine, however a curved one works magic here.

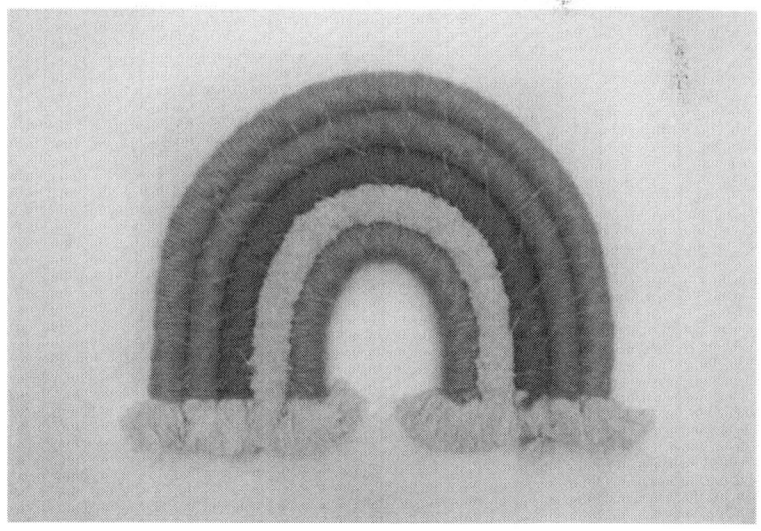

Step Five

Finishing your Rainbow

Take your comb and brush out the unwrapped 20mm rope that is at the bottom of your rainbow. The fluffier the better! Snip to suit your desired look.

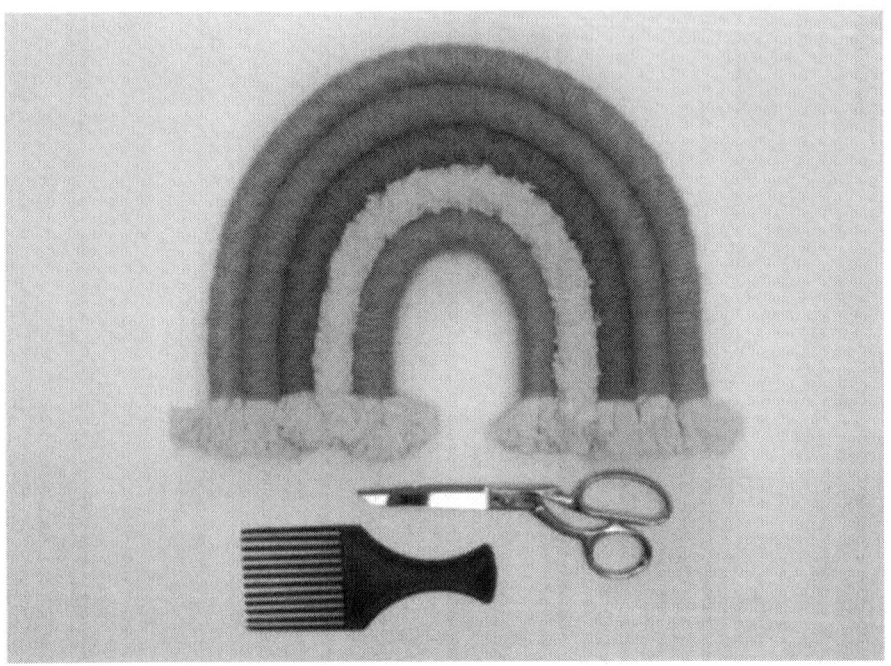

If you wish, sew a small split ring at the back of your rainbow to hang. ***And that's it!***What a beautiful creation you've crafted. What colour will you do next!?

Macrame Christmas Patterns

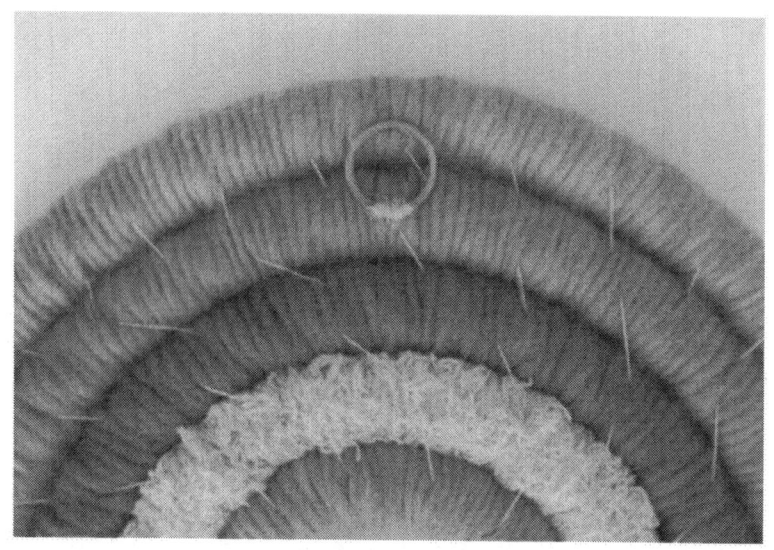

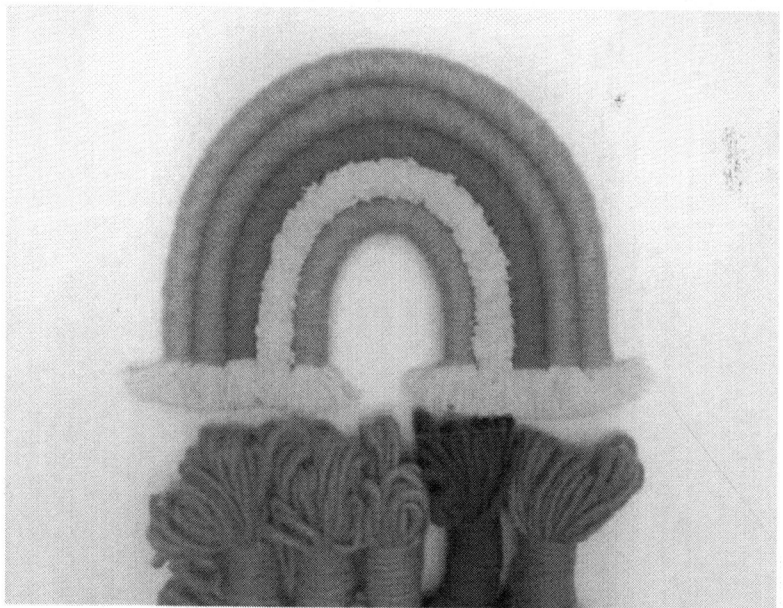

DIY Macrame Christmas Tree Ornament

Cut 6 pieces of rope, not 8 pieces. Sorry for the confusion!

Materials:

– 4mm 3 Ply Rope in White

– Metal Ring (0.5 inches)

– Gold Sewing Thread (optional)

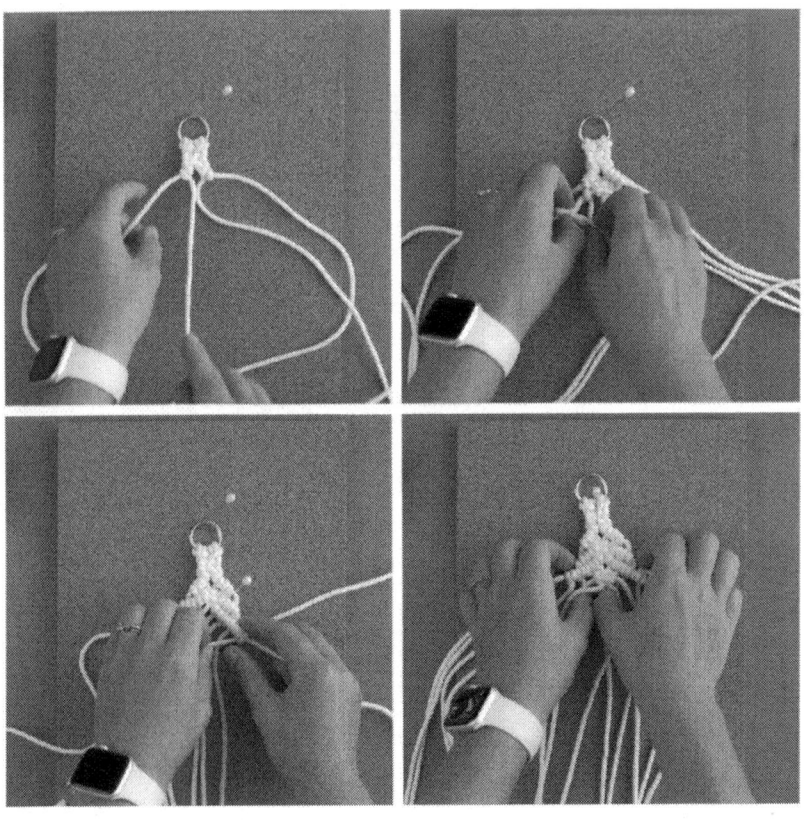

Macrame Christmas Patterns

Cut 6 pieces of rope, each piece is 4 ft long. Fold 2 pieces in half and attach to your ring using Lark's head knots. If you do not have a ring you could attach to another piece of rope.

With your 4 strands tie a square knot. Using the inside right strand as your filler cord tie a double half hitch knot. Repeat on the left side of your work.

Grab a new strand and fold it in half to find the centre. Bring the centre of the strand behind the strand on the right and tie a double half hitch knot. Repeat on the left side of your work.

Using the 4 middle strands tie a square knot. Use the strand on the left side of your square knot as your filler cord. Tie one double half hitch knot with the top strand from your final DHHK in your last row. Tie one more double half hitch knot with the filler cord from your last row of DHHK.

Using the inside right cord as your filler cord tie another row of double half hitch knots. Repeat on the left side of your work.

Grab a new strand and fold it in half to find the centre. Bring the centre of the strand behind the strand on the right and tie a double half hitch knot. Repeat that whole process on the left side of your work.

Macrame Christmas Patterns

Using the 4 middle strands tie a square knot.

Using the inside left strand as your filler cord tie another row of double half hitch knots. Repeat on the right side of your work.

Tie another row of double half hitch knots on both sides.

Tie one more square knot with the 4 middle strands.

We will tie one more row of double half hitch knots at the bottom of the tree. We will pick up strands as we go so that all of our strands end up on the middle.

Use the outside left strand as your filler cord and tie a double half hitch knot. Use both of the outside left strands as your filler cords and tie a double half hitch knot around both strands.

Pick up one extra strand as you go until you reach the middle of your work.

Repeat on the right side of your work.

You can hang your ornament on a tree with the ring or if you want it to hang down a bit more just add some thread to the top.

Finish it off with a gathering knot at the bottom or you can wrap some thin yarn, embroidery thread or sewing thread around the bottom.

Trim the ends however long you'd like.

Macrame Christmas Patterns

DIY Rainbow Macramé Earrings

Supplies Needed To Make Rainbow Macramé Earrings:

- **Rainbow Macramé Earring Findings**
- **1.5 mm Macramé Cord** (we prefer the Bobbiny brand)

Macrame Christmas Patterns

- **Jump Rings** and **Earring Wires**
- **Jewelry Pliers**
- Scissors
- **Bag Clip** (optional, but helpful!)
- **Comb** (optional)

Cut two pieces of macramé cord to size. Depending on how long you

Macrame Christmas Patterns

want your rainbows to hang, somewhere between 4-6 inches is a good size.

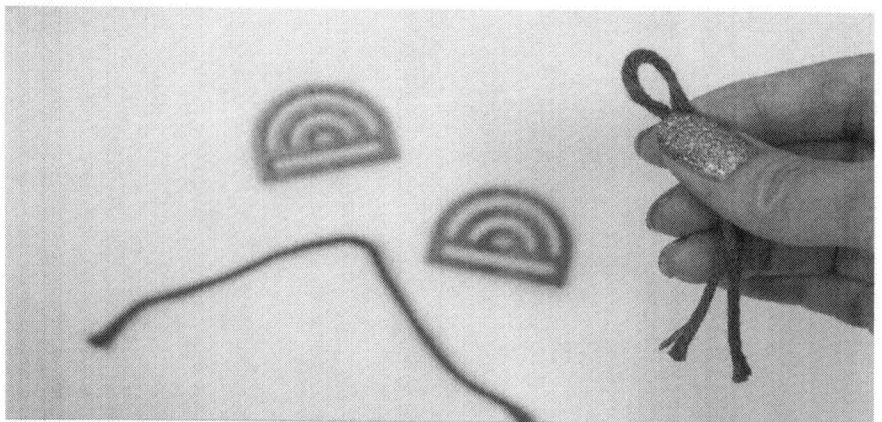

Loop one of the strings in half.

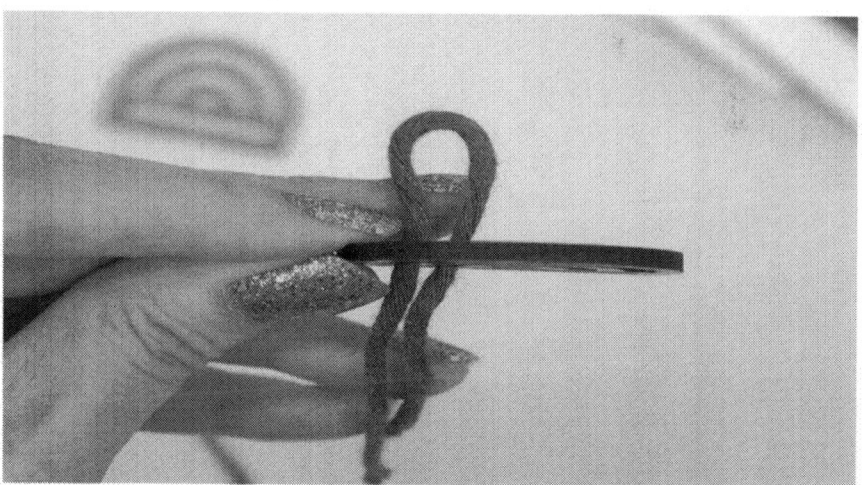

Thread the looped end through the horizontal opening in the

rainbow earring.

Bring the loop back under to the front, and thread the loose ends through it.

Gently and carefully tighten the loop (the wood earrings are rather sturdy, but they CAN break if you pull too hard on them!) and repeat the process with the other earring.

Repeat with additional colors as desired. The wood earring bases perfectly fit six colors of 1.5mm Bobbiny macramé cord, but could accommodate seven colors if you squeeze them tightly together.

As shown, the colors of cording that we used for this pair of earrings are: Wild Rose, Terracotta, Mustard, Eucalyptus Green, Teal, and Blackberry.

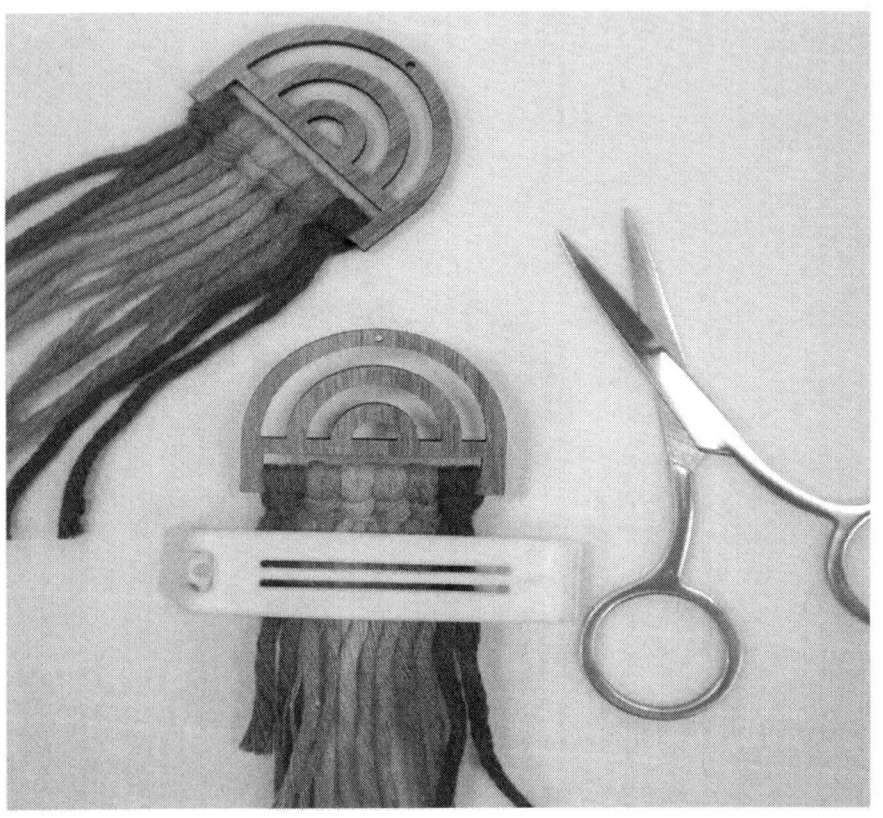

Next, it's time to trim your macramé cord, so grab a sharp pair of scissors.

Using a bag clip to hold the cording together helps to keep things straight and serves as a useful measuring tool to keep the earrings even.

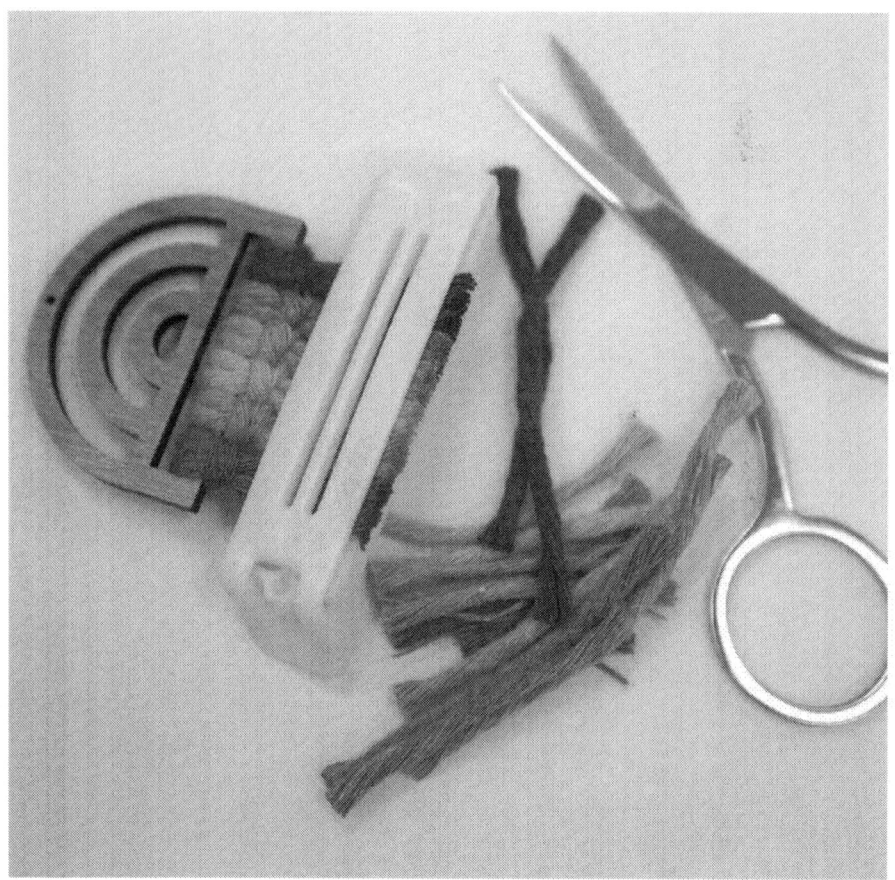

Trim your earrings as long or as short as you desire.

Macrame Christmas Patterns

You can leave the earrings with the cording intact as shown, or you can opt to fringe the cording. It looks great both ways, though you should be aware that over time, the cording may eventually start to fray on its own even if you don't choose to fringe it.

To fringe the cording, use an inexpensive comb with fairly tight teeth.

Being careful to avoid the knots, gently run the comb through the cording to untwist and separate the single strands.

Macrame Christmas Patterns

You can see the difference between a fringed/combed earring on the left and a corded earring on the right.

Macrame Christmas Patterns

Finally, use your jewelry pliers to attach the earring hardware (use two jump rings and an earring wire for each earring).

Macrame Christmas Patterns

Easy peasy and SUPER cute, don't you think!? These rainbow earrings would make a fantastic (and inexpensive!) homemade DIY gift idea!

Printed in Great Britain
by Amazon